Plug & Play Cowls™

Annie's

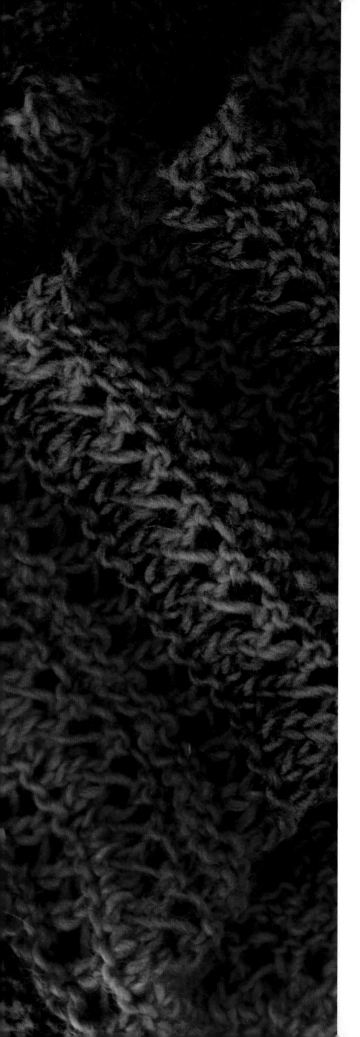

This is not your average stitch dictionary! We offer 6 cowls and 50 stitch patterns that give you unlimited options to inspire and excite you for years to come. We promise you'll never make the same cowl twice!

Most stitch dictionaries are a collection of stitch patterns—beautiful and fun to look through, but not necessarily useful as a guide on how to use the stitches presented. This book offers a clever new take on the timeless tradition of stitch dictionaries. This compilation doesn't just provide stitch patterns; it's designed to easily show you how to use them to create a cowl that suits your personal style.

Maybe you like the look of the Roman Stripe Moebius cowl, but you would like to make it in a different stitch pattern. Look for another pattern with the "reversible" symbol, which tells you that the pattern will be the same on both sides. You'll also find that some patterns allow you to offset the differences in stitch gauge by working a few rows of ribbing in between each patterned square.

We hope that this collection of stitch patterns and cowls will expand your knitting repertoire to help you find a new sense of creativity and confidence!

Table of Contents

The Essential Stitches

Even, Odd & Any Number of Stitches
9 Roman Lace, Roman Rib
10 Basic Faggoting, Moss Stitch
11 Roman Stitch, Seed Stitch
12 Twisted Rib

Multiple of 2 + 2
12 Linen Stitch
13 Rosette Stitch, Threaded Stitch

Multiple of 2 + 3
14 Fisherman's Rib

Multiple of 4
14 Cluster
15 Double Seed Stitch

Multiple of 4 + 2
15 Check
16 Cross-Stitch Rib, Swedish Check
17 Trinity Stitch

Multiple of 4 + 3
17 Mistake-Stitch Rib

Multiple of 4 + 6
18 Diagonal Scallop

Multiple of 4 + 8
18 Cat's Eye
19 Diagonal Madeira Lace

5-Stitch Panel
19 Zigzag Trellis

Multiple of 6 + 2
20 Acorns, Basket Weave
21 Spiral Rib, Italian Chain Rib
22 Little Knots, Swedish Blocks
23 Left Cable Rib, Right Cable Rib

Multiple of 6 + 8
24 Basket Lattice Cable
25 Interlocking Lattice

26 Hourglass Lace
27 Little Smocking

Multiple of 8 + 2
28 Chain-Link Cable
29 Mira Lace
30 Shadow Cable
31 Stars

Multiple of 8 + 10
32 Flower Meadow, Smocking

Multiple of 12
33 Aran Braid, Bamboo
34 Horseshoe Cable, Little Peacock
35 Diamonds
36 Pythagorean

Edgings
37 Flowing Lace Edging
38 Falling Leaves Edging
39 Meandering Lace Edging, Ruffle

Plug & Play Cowls
41 Lace Sampler
44 Roman Stripe Moebius
46 Textured Sampler Cowl
50 Cabled Cowl
54 Pleated Scarflette
57 Lace Shoulderette

General Information
4 Build Your Own Cowl
60 Knitting Basics
62 Special Techniques
63 Photo Index

The Essential Stitches, page 8

Textured Sampler Cowl, page 46

Build Your Own Cowl

Whether you have a cowl shape in mind, a couple of skeins to use up, or a cool stitch pattern to try, the design process starts with three elements: shape, yarn and a stitch pattern.

Shape

Deep or shallow, narrow or wide, multiple or single wrap, with a twist or without, hug the shoulders or hug the neck—the options for cowl shapes are endless. Browse Pinterest, look at magazines, search Ravelry, and of course, look through the patterns in this book!

Scribble down the measurements (length and width, depth and circumference) of shapes you like. Use something you already own as a template, or hold a tape measure to your body in front of a mirror to see what works for you.

Yarn

Cowls are a wonderful way to use up an extra ball or two in your stash. But like scarves, they can use more yarn than you think. A close-fitting neck warmer can take as little as 100 yards (if using big lacy stitches!), while a long, wide infinity scarf can take as much 800 (or more, if knitting cable patterns).

Check how many yards you have of your chosen yarn and compare it to the requirements of similar projects. Leave yourself some wiggle room so you don't run out of yarn, measuring your project as you knit it to double-check. If you have two balls of yarn and your fabric measures 8 inches after using up the first ball, you will run out of yarn before finishing the 20-inch cowl that you planned. Have a backup plan; you could shorten the piece, work an edging in a contrasting-color yarn, or rip back and make your fabric narrower.

Stitch Pattern

Stitch patterns are what give knitted fabric its texture, its unique appearance and its character. This book is chock-full of unique and interesting patterns to try! Each chapter is organized by the number of stitches in each pattern repeat, which makes it easy to substitute and combine patterns.

What's a pattern repeat? A pattern repeat is a group of stitches (knits, purls, increases, decreases and other stitch manipulations) that repeats across the length and width of the fabric. The number of stitches and rows in each group is said to be its repeat. For example, seed stitch has a 2-stitch repeat ("multiple of 2 sts" notation in the stitch instructions) and a 2-row repeat. Linen stitch also repeats every 2 stitches, but has a 4-row repeat.

LINEN ST CHART

Sometimes a pattern repeat is not symmetrical. When repeats are lined up next to one another, either as stitches or rows, one end does not appear the same as the other; in these cases, we can't say a pattern is simply a multiple of 4 stitches. The extra stitches that provide visual balance must be included in the instructions and are the "+" numbers you see in repeat notations. For example, when worked flat, 2 x 2 rib is a "multiple of 4 sts + 2." The last 2 knit stitches balance the 2 knit stitches at the beginning of the row. You can see the visual balance in the instructions: "k2, *p2, k2; rep from * to end." The same principle holds for row repeats.

Balancing stitches and rows can almost always be eliminated if you plan on working in the round or grafting ends together. To check your pattern, chart it on a paper strip and bring the sides or ends together—how do the pattern stitches or rows best fit together?

Shape, Yarn & Stitch Pattern: Now Swatch!

Cast on 4 to 6 inches' worth of stitches (see Nuts & Bolts), and make a swatch 4 to 6 inches tall; in other words, knit a piece of fabric that's big enough to tell you how your finished cowl might look and feel. Experiment with cast-on and bound-off edgings and try different selvage treatments on either side of the swatch.

While you swatch, think about construction methods:

Do you want to work in the round? Is the stitch pattern simple to convert? What about working flat, and grafting the ends together—or button, zip or tie the ends together? What does the pattern look like on its side? Should you work lengthwise (lots of stitches, fewer rows) or widthwise (fewer stitches, many rows)? Is the stitch pattern reversible—would it lend itself to a being a moebius? Do you want to sew one end to the opposite edge, as with the Lace Sampler on page 41?

The time you spend swatching will fly by as you ponder the possibilities.

Nuts & Bolts

Yarn labels are your starting point; they almost always include "suggested gauge" information. This is the number of stitches and rows the average knitter will use in a 4-inch square to make a sweater-appropriate fabric in stockinette stitch (for example, 20 sts and 28 rows); the label also suggests a needle size to achieve this gauge with the yarn.

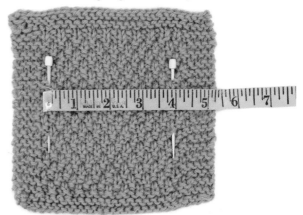

Reduce the suggested gauge numbers down to the number of stitches and rows per inch (SPI) by dividing the numbers by 4:

20 sts ÷ 4 inches = 5 sts per 1 inch (5 SPI)

This number is the stockinette stitch gauge of the yarn. To make a stockinette stitch swatch 6 inches wide, multiply the SPI by the desired number of inches:

5 SPI x 6 inches = 30 sts

This rough number needs to be adjusted based on the stitch pattern repeat. Let's use the Mira Lace (multiple of 8 sts + 2) pattern on page 29 as an example:

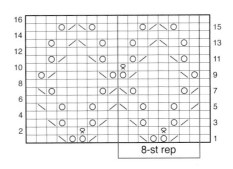

MIRA LACE CHART

30 sts ÷ 8 sts per repeat = 3 full repeats, with 6 sts left over

3 repeats x 8 sts per repeat = 24 sts

24 repeat sts + 2 balancing sts = 26 sts

OR, bump up the swatch size by 1 repeat:

4 repeats x 8 sts per repeat = 32 sts

32 repeat sts + 2 balancing sts = 34 sts

Casting on either 26 or 34 stitches will produce a visually balanced swatch in the chosen stitch pattern. Add extra stitches for any edgings you want to try, and cast on.

The same math applies vertically to row repeats. The nice thing about rows? You can usually just knit more of them to make your piece long enough.

Once you're done with your swatch, wash and block it.

Do you like the fabric that you've made? If yes, you're good; you just need to work the math for your desired measurements (see Build Your Own Cowl on page 7) using the actual gauge. However, if you want denser fabric, work another swatch using smaller needles. And if you think that a looser fabric would be better for the cowl that you have in mind, swatch again using larger needles. Once you get a fabric that you like, determine the gauge and go on to the next section.

Edges, Edgings, Bands & Closures

Sometimes the stitch pattern itself creates a wonderful top or bottom edge for a cowl, pulling the fabric up like drapes or causing it to zig and zag. Sometimes, a pretty cast-on or bind-off can do double-duty, creating not merely the first or last row of stitches but also edging the top and bottom in an interesting way.

And sometimes the edging is the star of the piece (see Pleated Scarflette on page 54), and the rest merely supports it. In such cases, when an edging abuts a stitch pattern or when two stitch patterns meet, you may need to change the number of stitches on the needle to accommodate the smaller or larger stitch counts required by different pattern repeats. Using a couple rows of garter stitch or reverse stockinette stitch as a transition can camouflage any necessary increases or decreases. You can also add edgings separately by either picking up stitches to work outward, grafting a separately worked piece to live stitches, or sewing.

You can work your selvage stitches (extra stitches at each side of a piece) in a variety of ways: You can slip them or work them in garter stitch or rib, or any other flat pattern that will keep the edge of a rolling fabric flat (see Textured Sampler Cowl on page 46); alternatively, you can work edge stitches in stockinette stitch to deliberately roll the edge of a flat fabric (see Cabled Cowl on page 50).

Similar tricks can be used to create design elements that will separate stitch patterns worked side by side. For example, the patterns in the Lace Sampler are divided by 5-stitch panels that combine 3 stitches of faggoting bordered on each side by 1-stitch purl channels. These panels frame the patterns to focus attention on them.

Finally, use bands and closures to turn rectangular pieces into circular cowls. Buttonholes and bands can close a cowl just like they close a cardigan: pick up stitches on each end and work a rib or garter band; insert buttonholes on one of the bands and sew buttons on the other, and you're done. Or use a feature of the stitch pattern itself as a buttonhole (eyelet and lace patterns need no additional buttonholes!) or to hide a buttonhole (see Cabled Cowl). I-cord ties and button loops can also be added afterward (see Pleated Scarflette) and make it easy to make adjustments for fit.

Revisit your cowl diagram, adding any edgings and closures, and notes on measurements.

Build Your Own Cowl

You've picked out your yarn and made a swatch in your chosen stitch pattern. Now it's time to pull all the pieces together and build your cowl pattern.

Using the same math used for your swatch, convert the inches on your cowl diagram to approximate numbers of stitches and rows.

For example, the Roman Stripe Moebius (see page 44) is 12 inches wide and 40 inches long. The Roman Stripe swatch knits up to 2.5 stitches per inch and 4 rows per inch.

How many stitches should be cast on? 12 inches x 2.5 sts/inch = 30 stitches

How many rows should be worked? 40 inches x 4 rows/inch = 160 rows.

Refine the rough stitch and row numbers to take pattern repeats and balancing stitches into account.

Roman Stripe requires an even number of stitches and has no balancing stitches.

Roman Stripe repeats every 14 rows. To make the pattern repeats match after twisting, we need to work an extra half repeat (7 rows).

160 rows/14 rows per repeat = 11.4 times.

14 rows x 11 repeats = 154 rows + 7 rows (half repeat) = 161 rows

Since knitting stretches and contracts, the extra row won't increase our length significantly.

Add stitches (or rows) for selvages, edgings, bands, and pattern separators or insertions.

There is an extra selvage stitch added on each side, since edge stitches turn to the side, for a total of 32 stitches.

The last half-repeat ends on a Row 5, leaving the grafting row and the cast-on row to act as the 2 knit rows in the middle of the pattern.

Cast on and knit!

Tips

Keep it simple by working your cowl in just one pattern (see Roman Stripe Moebius) or separate the patterns into sections worked one after another (see Textured Sampler Cowl).

Row gauge is crucial when working stitch patterns side by side. Swatch them side by side, or measure very carefully to check rows per inch.

When converting stitch patterns from flat to circular, remember that you will always be working on the right side of the piece. Wrong-side rows must be converted; knits become purls and purls become knits.

Inches must match inches! Edging and band patterns have gauge too, so test them on your main pattern swatch.

Charts are useful visual tools to see changes necessary for converting a flat pattern to circular. It might be as easy as just working all chart rows from right to left.

Have fun. After all, it's just a cowl!

The Essential Stitches

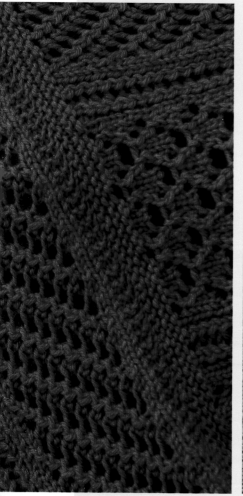
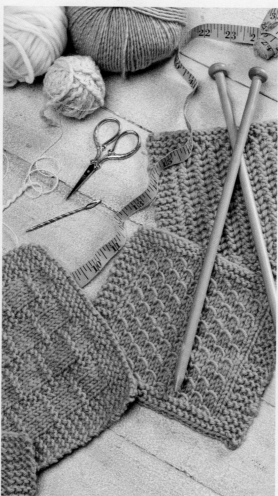

In the following section, you'll be introduced to an unlimited combination of stitch patterns that you can make as stand-alone stitch squares to learn new stitches, or you'll have endless hours of enjoyment applying them to the accompanying cowl patterns that begin on page 41. You'll never run out of possibilities.

Roman Lace

Roman Lace (any number of sts)

Note: St count will inc on Rows 1 and 8 and dec back to original count on Rows 3 and 10.

Row 1 (RS): *Yo, k1; rep from * to end.

Row 2: Purl.

Row 3: *K2tog; rep from * end.

Rows 4 and 5: *Yo, k2tog; rep from * to end.

Rows 6 and 7: Knit.

Rows 8–14: Rep Rows 1–7.

Rep Rows 1–14 for pat.

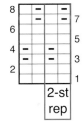

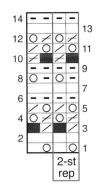

STITCH KEY

☐	K on RS, p on WS
−	P on RS, k on WS
O	Yo
╱	K2tog on RS
╱	K2tog on WS
■	No stitch

ROMAN LACE CHART

Roman Rib

Roman Rib (even number of sts)

Row 1 (RS): Knit.

Row 2: Purl.

Rows 3 and 4: *K1, p1; rep from * to end.

Row 5: Knit.

Row 6: Purl.

Rows 7 and 8: *P1, k1; rep from * to end.

Rep Rows 1–8 for pat.

STITCH KEY

☐	K on RS, p on WS
−	P on RS, k on WS

ROMAN RIB CHART

Basic Faggoting

Basic Faggoting (even number of sts)

Row 1: *Yo, ssk; rep from * to end.

Rep Row 1 for pat.

BASIC FAGGOTING CHART

Note: All rows are worked the same.

STITCH KEY	
⊡	Yo
⧄	Ssk on RS
⧅	Ssk on WS

Moss Stitch

Moss St (even number of sts)

Rows 1 (RS) and 2: *K1, p1; rep from * to end.

Rows 3 and 4: *P1, k1; rep from * to end.

Rep Rows 1–4 for pat.

MOSS ST CHART

STITCH KEY	
☐	K on RS, p on WS
⊟	P on RS, k on WS

Roman Stitch Seed Stitch

Roman St (even number of sts)

Rows 1 and 3 (RS): Knit.

Rows 2 and 4: Purl.

Row 5: *K1, p1; rep from * to end.

Row 6: *P1, k1; rep from * to end.

Rep Rows 1–6 for pat.

Seed St (odd number of sts)

Note: For even number of sts, skip the last k1 on Row 1.

Row 1: K1, *p1, k1; rep from * to end.

Row 2: Knit the purl sts and purl the knit sts.

Rep Row 2 for pat.

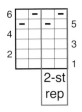

ROMAN ST CHART

SEED ST CHART

STITCH KEY
- ☐ K on RS, p on WS
- ⊟ P on RS, k on WS

STITCH KEY
- ☐ K on RS, p on WS
- ⊟ P on RS, k on WS

Twisted Rib

Twisted Rib (even number of sts)
All rows: *K1-tbl, p1; rep from * to end.

Linen Stitch

Linen St (multiple of 2 sts + 2)
Rows 1 and 3 (WS): Purl.

Row 2 (RS): K1, *sl 1 pwise wyif, k1; rep from * to last st, k1.

Row 4: K2, *sl 1 pwise wyif, k1; rep from * to end.

Rep Rows 1–4 for pat.

TWISTED RIB CHART

STITCH KEY
- ☐ K on RS, p on WS
- ⊟ P on RS, k on WS
- ⊠ K1-tbl on RS
- ⊠ K1-tbl on WS

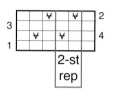

LINEN ST CHART

STITCH KEY
- ☐ K on RS, p on WS
- ⊻ Sl 1 pwise wyif

Rosette Stitch

Rosette St (multiple of 2 sts + 2)

Rows 1 and 3 (RS): Knit.

Row 2: *P2tog and leave sts on LH needle, k2tog the same 2 sts and slip from LH needle; rep from * to end.

Row 4: P1, *p2tog and leave sts on LH needle, k2tog the same 2 sts and slip from LH needle; rep from * to last st, p1.

Rep Rows 1–4 for pat.

ROSETTE ST CHART

STITCH KEY
☐ K on RS, p on WS
⟋⟍ (P2tog, k2tog) in same 2 sts

Threaded Stitch

Threaded St (multiple of 2 sts + 2)

Note: 2 needle sizes are used, one 3 sizes larger than other. Use larger needle to cast on.

Row 1 (RS): With smaller needle, knit.

Rows 2 and 4: With larger needle, purl.

Row 3: With smaller needle, *insert RH needle pwise through first st, knit 2nd st and leave on needle, knit first st tbl, slide both sts off LH needle; rep from * to end.

Row 5: With smaller needle, k1, *insert RH needle pwise through first st, knit 2nd st and leave on needle, knit first st tbl, slide both sts off LH needle; rep from * to last st, k1.

Rep Rows 2–5 for pat.

THREADED ST CHART

Note: Work Rows 1, 3 & 5 with smaller needle; work Rows 2 & 4 with larger needle.

STITCH KEY
☐ K on RS, p on WS
⧖ Insert RH needle pwise through first st, knit 2nd st and leave on needle, knit first st tbl, slide both sts off LH needle

Fisherman's Rib

Special Abbreviation

Knit 1 in row below (k1b): Insert RH needle kwise into st directly below first st on LH needle and draw up a loop, sl st from LH needle.

Fisherman's Rib (multiple of 2 sts + 3)

Row 1 (RS): K1, *p1, k1; rep from * to end.

Row 2: P1, *k1b, p1: rep from * to end.

Row 3: K1, *p1, k1b; rep from * to last 2 sts, p1, k1.

Rep Rows 2 and 3 for pat.

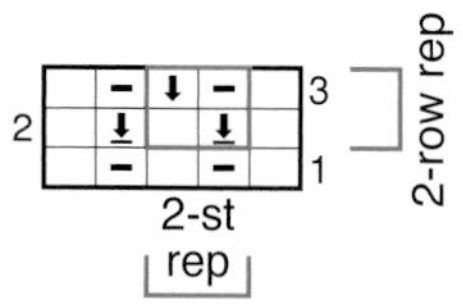

FISHERMAN'S RIB CHART

STITCH KEY

- K on RS, p on WS
- P on RS, k on WS
- K1b on RS
- K1b on WS

Cluster

Cluster (multiple of 4 sts)

Row 1 (RS): *K3tog, (p1, k1, p1) in next st; rep from * to end.

Row 2: *K3, p1; rep from * to end.

Row 3: *K1, p3; rep from * to end.

Row 4: Knit.

Row 5: *(P1, k1, p1) in next st, k3tog; rep from * to end.

Row 6: *P1, k3; rep from * to end.

Row 7: *P3, k1; rep from * to end.

Row 8: Knit.

Rep Rows 1–8 for pat.

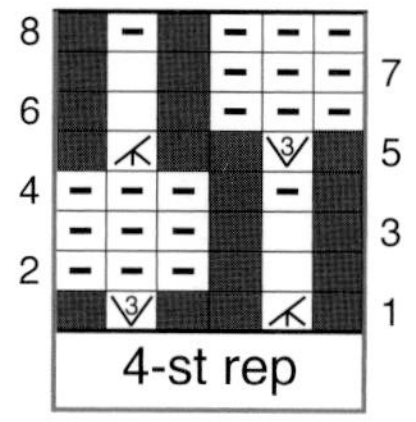

CLUSTER CHART

STITCH KEY

- K on RS, p on WS
- P on RS, k on WS
- K3tog
- (P1, k1, p1) in 1 st
- No st

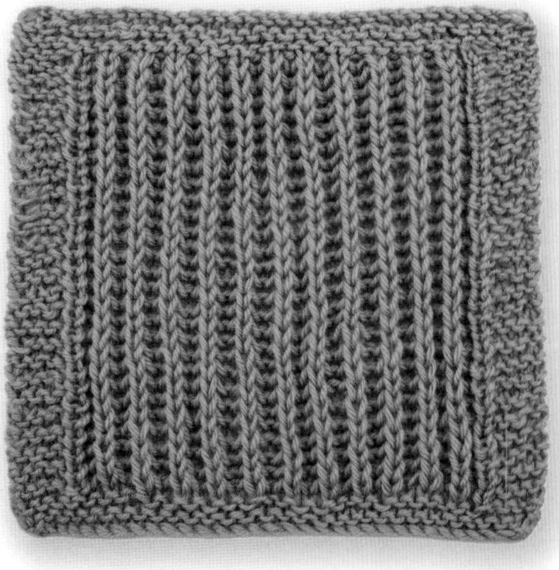

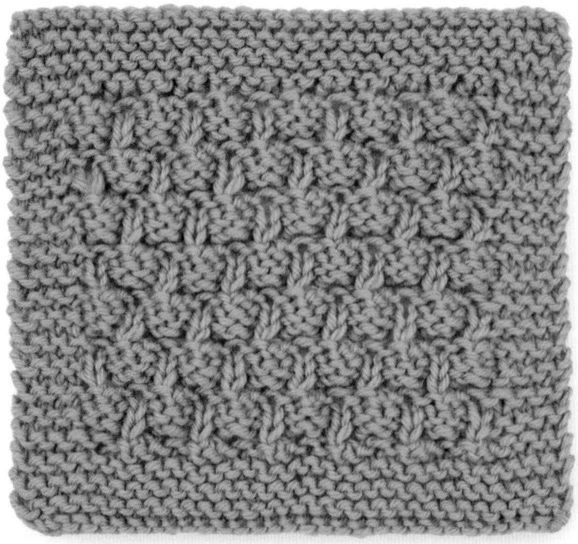

Double Seed Stitch

Double Seed St (multiple of 4 sts)

Rows 1 and 2: *K2, p2; rep from * to end.

Rows 3 and 4: *P2, k2; rep from * to end.

Rep Rows 1–4 for pat.

DOUBLE SEED ST CHART

STITCH KEY
☐ K on RS, p on WS
⊟ P on RS, k on WS

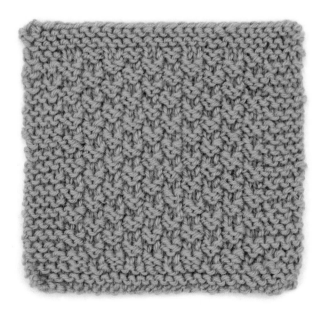

Check

Check (multiple of 4 sts + 2)

Row 1 (RS): K2, *p2, k2; rep from * to end.

Row 2: P2, *k2, p2; rep from * to end.

Rows 3 and 4: Knit.

Row 5: Rep Row 2.

Row 6: Rep Row 1.

Rows 7 and 8: Knit.

Rep Rows 1–8 for pat.

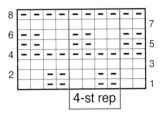

CHECK CHART

STITCH KEY
☐ K on RS, p on WS
⊟ P on RS, k on WS

Cross-Stitch Rib

Cross-Stitch Rib (multiple of 4 sts +2)

Row 1 (RS): P2, *skip first st, knit 2nd st, then knit first st, slip both sts from needle, p2; rep from * to end.

Row 2: K2, *p2, k2; rep from * to end.

Rep Rows 1 and 2 for pat.

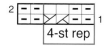

CROSS-STITCH RIB CHART

STITCH KEY
☐ K on RS, p on WS
− P on RS, k on WS
⋈ Skip first st, knit 2nd st, then knit first st; slip both sts from needle

Swedish Check

Swedish Check (multiple of 4 sts + 2)

Rows 1 and 5 (RS): Knit all sts tbl.

Rows 2 and 6: Purl.

Row 3: K2-tbl, *p2, k2-tbl; rep from * to end.

Row 4: P2, *k2, p2; rep from * to end.

Row 7: P2, *k2-tbl, p2; rep from * to end.

Row 8: K2, *p2, k2; rep from * to end.

Rep Rows 1–8 for pat.

SWEDISH CHECK CHART

STITCH KEY
☐ K on RS, p on WS
− P on RS, k on WS
৭ K1-tbl

Trinity Stitch

Trinity St (multiple of 4 sts + 2)

Rows 1 and 3 (RS): Purl.

Row 2: K1, *(k1, p1, k1) in next st, p3tog; rep from * to last st, k1

Row 4: K1, *p3tog, (k1, p1, k1) in next st; rep from * to last st, k1.

Rep Rows 1–4 for pat.

Mistake-Stitch Rib

Mistake-St Rib (multiple of 4 sts + 3)
Row 1: *K2, p2; rep from * to last 3 sts, k2, p1.

Rep Row 1 for pat.

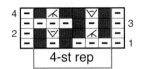

TRINITY ST CHART

STITCH KEY
−	P on RS, k on WS
▽	(K1, p1, k1) in 1 st
⋌	P3tog on WS
■	No st

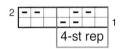

MISTAKE-ST RIB CHART

STITCH KEY
□	K on RS, p on WS
−	P on RS, k on WS

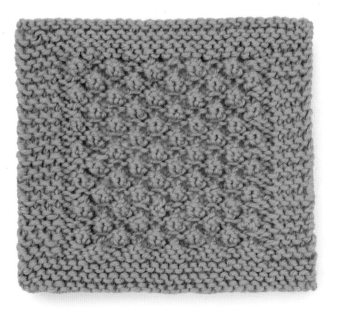

Diagonal Scallop

Diagonal Scallop (multiple of 4 sts + 6)

Rows 1 and 3 (WS): Purl.

Row 2: K1, *insert RH needle from back to front under running thread between sts and lift onto RH needle, k2, pass lifted st over these 2 sts, k2; rep from * to last st, k1.

Row 4: K3, *insert RH needle from back to front under running thread between sts and lift onto RH needle, k2, pass lifted st over these 2 sts, k2; rep from * to last 3 sts, insert RH needle from back to front under running thread between sts and lift onto RH needle, k2, pass lifted st over these 2 sts, k1.

Rep Rows 1–4 for pat.

STITCH KEY

☐ K on RS, p on WS

⊏⊐ Insert RH needle from back to front under running thread between sts and lift onto RH needle, k2, pass lifted st over these 2 sts

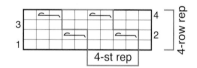

DIAGONAL SCALLOP CHART

Cat's Eye

Special Abbreviation

Double yarn over (2yo): Yo twice between sts; work (p1, k1) into 2yo loop on next row.

Cat's Eye (multiple of 4 sts + 8)

Row 1 (RS): K4, *2yo, k4; rep from * to end—2 sts inc per rep.

Row 2: P2, *p2tog, (p1, k1) in 2yo, p2tog; rep from * to last 2 sts, p2—2 sts dec per rep.

Row 3: K2, yo, *k4, 2yo; rep from * to last 6 sts, k4, yo, k2—2 sts inc per rep.

Row 4: P3, *p2tog twice, (p1, k1) in 2yo; rep from * to last 7 sts, p2tog twice, p3—2 sts dec per rep.

Rep Rows 1–4 for pat.

STITCH KEY

☐ K on RS, p on WS

– K on WS

○ Yo

╱ P2tog on WS

■ No st

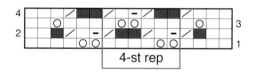

CAT'S EYE CHART

Diagonal Madeira Lace

Diagonal Madeira Lace (multiple of 4 sts + 8)

Row 1 (RS): K2, *yo, sk2p, yo, k1; rep from * to last 2 sts, k2.

Row 2 and all WS rows: Purl.

Row 3: K2, *k1, yo, sk2p, yo; rep from * to last 2 sts, k2.

Row 5: K1, k2tog, *yo, k1, yo, sk2p; rep from * to last 5 sts, yo, k1, yo, ssk, k2.

Row 7: K2, k2tog, *yo, k1, yo, sk2p; rep from * to last 4 sts, yo, k1, yo, ssk, k1.

Row 8: Purl.

Rep Rows 1–8 for pat.

STITCH KEY
- ☐ K on RS, p on WS
- ○ Yo
- ⤬ Sk2p
- ⟋ K2tog
- ⟍ Ssk

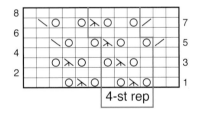

DIAGONAL MADEIRA LACE CHART

Zigzag Trellis

Zigzag Trellis (5-st panel)

Row 1 (RS): P1, ssk, yo, k1, p1.

Row 2: K1, p2tog, yo, p1, k1.

Rep Rows 1 and 2 for pat.

STITCH KEY
- ☐ K on RS, p on WS
- – P on RS, k on WS
- ○ Yo
- ⟋ P2tog on WS
- ⟍ Ssk on RS

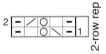

ZIGZAG TRELLIS PANEL CHART

Acorns

Acorns (multiple of 6 sts + 2)

Rows 1 and 3 (RS): K1, *k3, p3; rep from * to last st, k1.

Rows 2 and 4: P1, *k3, p3; rep from * to last st, p1.

Row 5: K1, *yo, k3tog, yo, k3; rep from * to last st, k1.

Rows 6 and 8: P1, *p3, k3; rep from * to last st, p1.

Row 7: K1, *p3, k3; rep from * to last st, k1.

Row 9: K1, *k3, yo, k3tog, yo; rep from * to last st, k1.

Row 10: Rep Row 2.

Rep Rows 3–10 for pat.

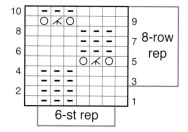

6-st rep

ACORNS CHART

Basket Weave

Basket Weave (multiple of 6 sts + 2)

Rows 1 and 3 (RS): K1, *k3, p3; rep from * to last st, k1.

Rows 2 and 4: P1, *k3, p3; rep from * to last st, p1.

Rows 5 and 7: K1, *p3, k3; rep from * to last st, k1.

Rows 6 and 8: P1, *p3, k3; rep from * to last st, p1.

Rep Rows 1–8 for pat.

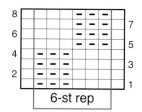

6-st rep

BASKET WEAVE CHART

STITCH KEY

☐	K on RS, p on WS
−	P on RS, k on WS
○	Yo
⊼	K3tog

STITCH KEY

☐	K on RS, p on WS
−	P on RS, k on WS

Spiral Rib

Special Abbreviation

Right Twist (RT): K2tog and leave on needle; insert RH needle into first st and k1; slip both sts from needle tog.

Spiral Rib (multiple of 6 sts + 2)

Rows 1 and 3 (WS): K2, *p4, k2; rep from * to end.

Row 2 (RS): P2, *RT twice, p2; rep from * to end.

Row 4: P2, *K1, RT, k1, p2; rep from * to end.

Rep Rows 1–4 for pat.

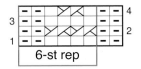

SPIRAL RIB CHART

STITCH KEY	
☐	K on RS, p on WS
⊟	P on RS, k on WS
⧅⧄	RT

Italian Chain Rib

Special Abbreviation

Double yarn over (2yo): Yo twice between sts. On next row, purl in front and back of 2yo loop.

Italian Chain Rib (multiple of 6 sts + 2)

Note: This pat looks good on both sides.

Row 1 (WS): K2, *p4, k2; rep from * to end.

Row 2 (RS): P2, *k2tog, 2yo, ssk, p2; rep from * to end.

Row 3: K2, *p1, purl into front and back of 2yo, p1, k2; rep from * to end.

Row 4: P2, *yo, ssk, k2tog, yo, p2; rep from * to end.

Rep Rows 1–4 for pat.

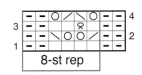

ITALIAN CHAIN RIB CHART

STITCH KEY	
☐	K on RS, p on WS
⊟	P on RS, k on WS
◯	Yo
╱	K2tog
╲	Ssk
⊗	P1-tbl on WS

Little Knots

Little Knots (multiple of 6 sts + 2)

Note: *Do not twist running thread when knitting into it; loop should rem open.*

Rows 1 and 3 (WS): Purl.

Row 2 (RS): K1, *k3, knit into running thread between st on RH needle and st on LH needle, sk2p, knit into running thread; rep from * to last st, end k1.

Row 4: K1, *knit into running thread, sk2p, knit into running thread, k3; rep from * to last st, k1.

Rep Rows 1–4 for pat.

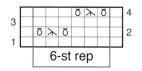

LITTLE KNOTS CHART

STITCH KEY
- ☐ K on RS, p on WS
- ⊙ Knit into running thread between st on RH needle and st on LH needle
- ⋉ Sk2p

Swedish Blocks

Swedish Blocks (multiple of 6 sts + 2)

Row 1 (RS): K2, *p4, k2; rep from * to end.

Row 2: P2, *k4, p2; rep from * to end.

Rows 3, 5 and 7: Rep Row 2.

Rows 4, 6 and 8: Rep Row 1.

Rep Rows 1–8 for pat.

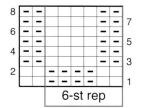

SWEDISH BLOCKS CHART

STITCH KEY
- ☐ K on RS, p on WS
- − P on RS, k on WS

Left Cable Rib

Special Abbreviation

2 over 2 Left Cross (2/2 LC): Sl 2 to cn and hold in front, k2, k2 from cn.

Left Cable Rib (multiple of 6 sts + 2)

Rows 1 and 3 (WS): K2, *p4, k2; rep from * to end.

Row 2 (RS): P2, *2/2 LC, p2; rep from * to end.

Row 4: P2, *k4, p2; rep from * to end.

Rep Rows 1–4 for pat.

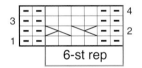

LEFT CABLE RIB CHART

Right Cable Rib

Special Abbreviation

2 over 2 Right Cross (2/2 RC): Sl 2 to cn and hold in back, k2, k2 from cn.

Right Cable Rib (multiple of 6 sts + 2)

Rows 1 and 3 (WS): K2, *p4, k2; rep from * to end.

Row 2 (RS): P2, *2/2 RC, p2; rep from * to end.

Row 4: P2, *k4, p2; rep from * to end.

Rep Rows 1–4 for pat.

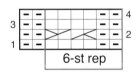

RIGHT CABLE RIB CHART

STITCH KEY
- ☐ K on RS, p on WS
- ⊟ P on RS, k on WS
- ⨝ 2/2 RC

Basket Lattice Cable

Special Abbreviations

2 over 2 Right Cross (2/2 RC): Sl 2 sts to cn and hold in back, k2, k2 from cn.

2 over 2 Left Cross (2/2 LC): Sl 2 sts to cn and hold in front, k2, k2 from cn.

2 over 1 Right Purl Cross (2/1 RPC): Sl 1 st to cn and hold in back, k2, p1 from cn.

2 over 1 Left Purl Cross (2/1 LPC): Sl 2 sts to cn and hold in front, p1, k2 from cn.

Basket Lattice Cable (multiple of 6 sts + 8)

Row 1 (WS): K2, *p4, k2; rep from * to end.

Row 2: P2, *2/2 RC, p2; rep from * to end.

Rows 3, 5 and 7: Knit the knit sts and purl the purl sts.

Row 4: P1, *2/1 RPC, 2/1 LPC; rep from * to last st, p1.

Row 6: P1, k2, p2, *2/2 LC, p2; rep from * to last 3 sts, k2, p1.

Row 8: P1, *2/1 LPC, 2/1 RPC; rep from * to last st, p1.

Rep Rows 1–8 for pat.

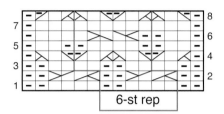

BASKET LATTICE CABLE CHART

STITCH KEY	
☐	K on RS, p on WS
−	P on RS, k on WS
⟩⟨	2/2 RC
⟨⟩	2/2 LC
⟋ ⟍	2/1 RPC
⟍ ⟋	2/1 LPC

Interlocking Lattice

Special Abbreviations

1 over 1 Right Cross (1/1 RC): Sl 1 to cn and hold in back, k1, then k1 from cn.

1 over 1 Left Cross (1/1 LC): Sl 1 to cn and hold in front, k1, then k1 from cn.

1 over 1 Right Purl Cross (1/1 RPC): Sl 1 to cn and hold in back, k1, then p1 from cn.

1 over 1 Left Purl Cross (1/1 LPC): Sl 1 to cn and hold in front, p1, then k1 from cn.

Interlocking Lattice (multiple of 6 sts + 8)

Row 1 (WS): K1, p1, *k4, p2; rep from * to last 6 sts, k4, p1, k1.

Row 2: P1, *1/1 LPC, p2, 1/1 RPC; rep from * to last st, p1.

Row 3 and all WS rows: Knit the knit sts and purl the purl sts.

Row 4: P2, *1/1 LPC, 1/1 RPC, p2; rep from * to end.

Row 6: P3, *1/1 RC, p4; rep from * to last 3 sts, p3.

Row 8: P2, *1/1 RPC, 1/1 LPC, p2; rep from * to end.

Row 10: P2, *1/1 LPC, 1/1 RPC, p2; rep from * to end.

Row 12: P3, *1/1 RC, p4; rep from * to last 3 sts, p3.

Row 14: P2, *1/1 RPC, 1/1 LPC, p2; rep from * to end.

Row 16: P1, *1/1 RPC, p2, 1/1 LPC; rep from * to last st, p1.

Row 18: 1/1 RPC, p4, *1/1 LC, p4; rep from * to last 2 sts, 1/1 LPC.

Row 20: K1, p4, *1/1 RPC, 1/1 LPC, p2; rep from * to last 3 sts, p2, k1.

Row 22: K1, p4, *1/1 LPC, 1/1 RPC, p2; rep from * to last 3 sts, p2, k1.

Row 24: 1/1 LPC, p4, *1/1 LC, p4; rep from * to last 2 sts, 1/1 RPC.

Rep Rows 1–24 for pat.

STITCH KEY	
☐	K on RS, p on WS
☐	P on RS, k on WS
⊠	1/1 LPC
⊠	1/1 RPC
⊠	1/1 RC
⊠	1/1 LC

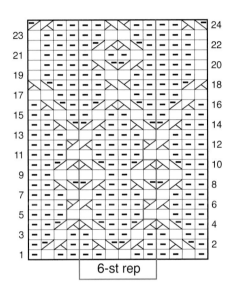

INTERLOCKING LATTICE CHART

6-st rep

Hourglass Lace

Special Abbreviation

Double yarn over (2yo): Yo twice between sts; work (k1, p1) into 2yo loop on next row.

Hourglass Lace (multiple of 6 sts + 8)

Row 1 (RS): K2, *yo, ssk, k2tog, yo, k2; rep from * to end.

Rows 2 and 6: Purl.

Row 3: K2, *k2tog, 2yo, ssk, k2; rep from * to end.

Row 4: P3, *(k1, p1) into 2yo, p4; rep from * to last 3 sts, p3.

Row 5: K1, *k2tog, yo, k2, yo, ssk; rep from * to last st, k1.

Row 7: K1, yo, *ssk, k2, k2tog, 2yo; rep from * to last 7 sts, ssk, k2, k2tog, yo, k1.

Row 8: P6, *(k1, p1) into 2yo, p4; rep from * to last 2 sts, p2.

Rep Rows 1–8 for pat.

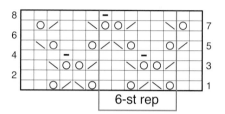

HOURGLASS LACE CHART

STITCH KEY	
☐	K on RS, p on WS
⊟	P on RS, k on WS
⊡	Yo
⧹	Ssk
⧸	K2tog

Little Smocking

Special Abbreviation

Wrap 2 (4): Sl 2 (4) sts to cn, wrap yarn around sts on cn once, k2 (4) from cn.

Little Smocking (multiple of 6 sts + 8)

Row 1 (RS): *P2, k4; rep from * to last 2 sts, p2.

Rows 2 and 4: *K2, p4; rep from * to last 2 sts, k2.

Row 3: *P2, Wrap 4; rep from * to last 2 sts, p2.

Row 5: K3, p2, *k4, p2; rep from * to last 3 sts, k3.

Row 6: P3, k2, *p4, k2; rep from * to last 3 sts, p3.

Row 7: K1, Wrap 2, *p2, Wrap 4; rep from * to last 5 sts, p2, Wrap 2, k1.

Row 8: P3, k2, *p4, k2; rep from * to last 3 sts, p3.

Rep Rows 1–8 for pat.

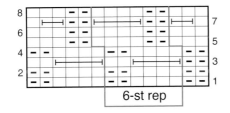

LITTLE SMOCKING CHART

STITCH KEY

☐ K on RS, p on WS

– P on RS, k on WS

|⊢⊣⊣⊣⊣⊣| Wrap 4

|⊢⊣| Wrap 2

Chain-Link Cable

Special Abbreviations

2 over 2 Right Cross Decrease (2/2 RC-Dec):
Sl 2 sts to cn and hold in back, sl next 2 sts to a 2nd cn and hold in front, k2tog, k2 from front cn, k2tog from back cn—2 sts dec.

2 over 2 Left Purl Cross Increase (2/2 LPC-Inc):
Sl 1 st to cn and hold in front, sl 2 sts to a 2nd cn and hold in back, pfb in next st, k2 from back cn, pfb in st from front cn—2 sts inc.

Purl in front and back (pfb): Purl in front and back of st.

Chain-Link Cable (multiple of 8 sts + 2)

Row 1 (RS): P2, *k2, p2; rep from * to end.

Row 2: K2, *p2, k2; rep from * to end.

Rows 3 and 4: Rep Rows 1 and 2.

Row 5: P2, *2/2 RC-Dec, p2; rep from * to end.

Row 6: K2, *p4, k2; rep from * to end.

Row 7: P2, *k4, p2; rep from * to end.

Row 8: K2, *2/2 LPC-Inc, k2; rep from * to end.

Rows 9–12: Rep [Rows 1 and 2] twice.

Rep Rows 1–12 for pat.

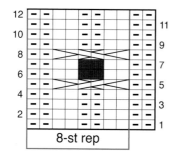

CHAIN-LINK CABLE CHART

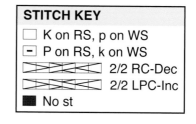

STITCH KEY	
☐	K on RS, p on WS
−	P on RS, k on WS
⨉	2/2 RC-Dec
⨉	2/2 LPC-Inc
■	No st

Mira Lace

Special Abbreviation

Double yarn over (2yo): Yo twice between sts. On next row, purl in front and back of 2yo loop.

Mira Lace (multiple of 8 sts + 2)

Row 1 (RS): K1, *k2, k2tog, 2yo, ssk, k2; rep from * to last st, k1.

Row 2 and all WS rows: Purl across, purling in front and back of each 2yo.

Row 3: K1, *k1, k2tog, yo, k2, yo, ssk, k1; rep from * to last st, k1.

Row 5: K1, *k2tog, k1, yo, k2, yo, k1, ssk; rep from * to last st, k1.

Row 7: K1, *k2tog, yo, k4, yo, ssk; rep from * to last st, k1.

Row 9: K1, *yo, ssk, k4, k2tog, yo; rep from * to last st, k1.

Row 11: K1, *k1, yo, ssk, k2, k2tog, yo, k1; rep from * to last st, k1.

Row 13: K1, *k1, yo, k1, ssk, k2tog, k1, yo, k1; rep from * to last st, k1.

Row 15: K1, *k2, yo, ssk, k2tog, yo, k2; rep from * to last st, k1.

Row 16: Purl across.

Rep Rows 1–16 for pat.

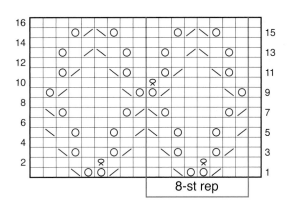

MIRA LACE CHART

8-st rep

STITCH KEY

☐	K on RS, p on WS
⊙	Yo
╱	K2tog
╲	Ssk
⊗	P1-tbl

Shadow Cable

Special Abbreviations

2 over 2 Right Cross (2/2 RC): Sl 2 sts to cn and hold in back, k2, k2 from cn.

2 over 2 Left Cross (2/2 LC): Sl 2 sts to cn and hold in front, k2, k2 from cn.

Shadow Cable (multiple of 8 sts + 2)

Row 1 and all WS rows: Purl.

Row 2 (RS): Knit.

Row 4: K1, *2/2 RC, k4; rep from * to last st, k1.

Row 6: Knit.

Row 8: K1, *k4; 2/2 LC; rep from * to last st, k1.

Rep Rows 1–8 for pat.

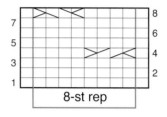

SHADOW CABLE CHART

STITCH KEY

☐	K on RS, p on WS
⤬	2/2 RC
⤬	2/2 LC

Stars

Special Abbreviation

Make 1 Left (M1L): Insert LH needle from front to back under horizontal strand between last st worked and next st on LH needle; knit through back of resulting loop.

Stars (multiple of 8 sts + 2)

Rows 1 and 3 (RS): K1, *[k2tog] twice, k4; rep from * to last st, k1.

Rows 2 and 4: P1, *p4, [k1, M1L] twice; rep from * to last st, p1.

Rows 5 and 7: K1, *k4, [k2tog] twice; rep from * to last st, k1.

Rows 6 and 8: P1, *[k1, M1L] twice, p4; rep from * to last st, p1.

Rep Rows 1–8 for pat.

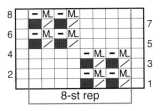

STARS CHART

STITCH KEY

☐	K on RS, p on WS
⊟	P on RS, k on WS
╱	K2tog
M̲	M1L
■	No stitch

Flower Meadow

Special Abbreviation

Make Flower (MF): K3tog, but leave sts on LH needle, knit first st again, then knit 2nd and 3rd sts tog, dropping the original sts from LH needle.

Flower Meadow (multiple of 8 sts + 10)

Rows 1 and 3 (RS): Knit.

Row 2 and all WS rows: Purl.

Row 5: K3, *MF, k5; rep from * to last 7 sts, MF, k4.

Rows 7 and 9: Knit.

Row 11: K7, *MF, k5; rep from * to last 3 sts, k3.

Row 12: Purl.

Rep Rows 1–12 for pat.

STITCH KEY
- ☐ K on RS, p on WS
- ☒ MF

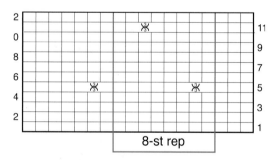

8-st rep

FLOWER MEADOW CHART

Smocking

Special Abbreviation

Smock 6: Insert RH needle from front to back between 6th and 7th sts on LH needle, draw a loop through and place on LH needle, then knit it tog with first st on LH needle, k1, p2, k2.

Smocking (multiple of 8 sts + 10)

Row 1 and all WS rows: K2, *p2, k2; rep from * to end.

Rows 2 and 6: P2, *k2, p2; rep from * to end.

Row 4: P2, *Smock 6, p2; rep from * to end.

Row 8: P2, k2, p2, *Smock 6, p2; rep from * to last 4 sts, k2, p2.

Rep Rows 1–8 for pat.

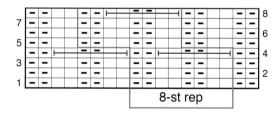

8-st rep

SMOCKING CHART

STITCH KEY
- ☐ K on RS, p on WS
- ⊟ P on RS, k on WS
- ⊞ Smock 6

Aran Braid

Special Abbreviations

2 over 2 Right Cross (2/2 RC): Sl 2 to cn and hold in back, k2, k2 from cn.

2 over 2 Left Cross (2/2 LC): Sl 2 to cn and hold in front, k2, k2 from cn.

Aran Braid (multiple of 12 sts)

Row 1 (WS): *K2, p8, k2; rep from * to end.

Row 2 (RS): *P2, [2/2 RC] twice, p2; rep from * to end.

Row 3: *K2, p8, k2; rep from * to end.

Row 4: *P2, k2, 2/2 LC, k2, p2; rep from * to end.

Rep Rows 1–4 for pat.

ARAN BRAID CHART

STITCH KEY
- ☐ K on RS, p on WS
- ⊟ P on RS, k on WS
- ⧖ 2/2 RC
- ⧖ 2/2 LC

Bamboo

Bamboo (multiple of 12 sts)

Row 1 and all RS rows: Knit.

Row 2: *K7, p4, k1; rep from * to end.

Row 4: *K1, p4, k2, p4, k1; rep from * to end.

Row 6: *K1, p4, k7; rep from * to end.

Row 8: Rep Row 4.

Rep Rows 1–8 for pat.

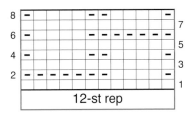

BAMBOO CHART

STITCH KEY
- ☐ K on RS, p on WS
- ⊟ P on RS, k on WS

Horseshoe Cable

Special Abbreviations

2 over 2 Right Cross (2/2 RC): Sl 2 to cn and hold in back, k2, k2 from cn.

2 over 2 Left Cross (2/2 LC): Sl 2 to cn and hold in front, k2, k2 from cn.

Horseshoe Cable (multiple of 12 sts)

Row 1 and all WS rows: *K2, p8, k2; rep from * to end.

Row 2 (RS): *P2, 2/2 RC, 2/2 LC, p2; rep from * to end.

Rows 4, 6 and 8: *P2, k8, p2; rep from * to end.

Rep Rows 1–8 for pat.

STITCH KEY
☐ K on RS, p on WS
– P on RS, k on WS
▨ 2/2 RC
▨ 2/2 LC

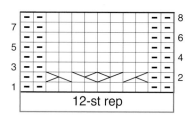

HORSESHOE CABLE CHART

12-st rep

Little Peacock

Little Peacock (multiple of 12 sts)

Row 1 (RS): Knit.

Row 2: Purl.

Row 3: *[K2tog] twice, [yo, k1] 4 times, [k2tog] twice; rep from * to end.

Row 4: Purl.

Row 5: Knit.

Row 6: Purl.

Rep Rows 3–6 for pat.

STITCH KEY
☐ K on RS, p on WS
╱ K2tog
◯ Yo

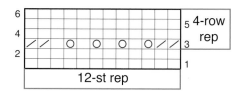

LITTLE PEACOCK CHART

4-row rep

12-st rep

Diamonds

Diamonds (multiple of 12 sts)

Note: This pattern is reversible, but the 2 sides will look somewhat different.

Row 1 (RS): *K2, p5, k2, p3; rep from * to end.

Row 2 and all WS rows: Knit the knit sts and purl the purl sts across.

Row 3 and 19: *P1, k2, p3, k2, p2, k1, p1; rep from * to end.

Row 5 and 17: *P2, k2, p1, k2, p2, k3; rep from * to end.

Row 7 and 15: *K1, p2, k3, p2, k2, p1, k1; rep from * to end.

Row 9 and 13: *K2, p2, k1, p2, k2, p3; rep from * to end.

Row 11: *P1, k2, p3, k2, p4; rep from * to end.

Row 20: Rep Row 2.

Rep Rows 1–20 for pat.

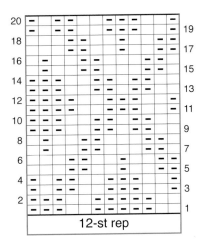

DIAMONDS CHART

STITCH KEY
☐ K on RS, p on WS
⊟ P on RS, k on WS

12-st rep

Alternative Side

Pythagorean

Pythagorean (multiple of 12 sts)

Rows 1 (RS) and 2: *P6, k6; rep from * to end.

Rows 3 and 4: *K1, p5, k5, p1; rep from * to end.

Rows 5 and 6: *K2, p4, k4, p2; rep from * to end.

Rows 7 and 8: *K3, p3; rep from * to end.

Rows 9 and 10: *K4, p2, k2, p4; rep from * to end.

Rows 11 and 12: *K5, p1, k1, p5; rep from * to end.

Rows 13 and 14: *K6, p6; rep from * to end.

Rows 15 and 16: *P6, k6; rep from * to end.

Rows 17 and 18: *P5, k1, p1, k5; rep from * to end.

Rows 19 and 20: *P4, k2, p2, k4; rep from * to end.

Rows 21 and 22: *P3, k3; rep from * to end.

Rows 23 and 24: *P2, k4, p4, k2; rep from * to end.

Rows 25 and 26: *P1, k5, p5, k1, rep from * to end.

Rows 27 and 28: *K6, p6; rep from * to end.

Rep Rows 1–28 for pat.

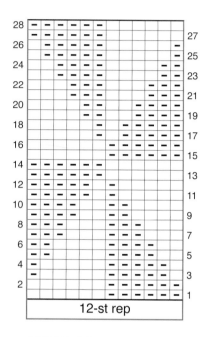

PYTHAGOREAN CHART

STITCH KEY
☐ K on RS, p on WS
⊟ P on RS, k on WS

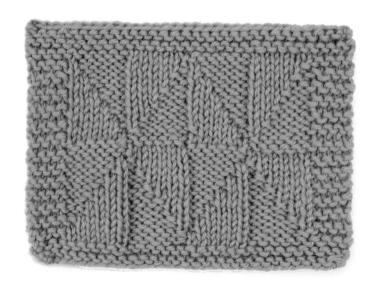

Flowing Lace Edging

Flowing Lace Edging (14 sts, inc to 19)

Cast on 14 sts.

Row 1 (WS): K2, yo, k2tog, k5, yo, k2tog, yo, k3—15 sts.

Row 2 and all RS rows: K1, yo, k2tog, knit to end.

Row 3: K2, yo, k2tog, k4, [yo, k2tog] twice, yo, k3—16 sts.

Row 5: K2, yo, k2tog, k3, [yo, k2tog] 3 times, yo, k3—17 sts.

Row 7: K2, yo, k2tog, k2, [yo, k2tog] 4 times, yo, k3—18 sts.

Row 9: K2, yo, k2tog, k1, [yo, k2tog] 5 times, yo, k3—19 sts.

Row 11: K2, yo, k2tog, k1, k2tog, [yo, k2tog] 5 times, k2—18 sts.

Row 13: K2, yo, k2tog, k2, k2tog, [yo, k2tog] 4 times, k2—17 sts.

Row 15: K2, yo, k2tog, k3, k2tog, [yo, k2tog] 3 times, k2—16 sts.

Row 17: K2, yo, k2tog, k4, k2tog, [yo, k2tog] twice, k2—15 sts.

Row 19: K2, yo, k2tog, k5, k2tog, yo, k2tog, k2—14 sts.

Row 20: K1, yo, k2tog, knit to end.

Rep Rows 1–20 for pat.

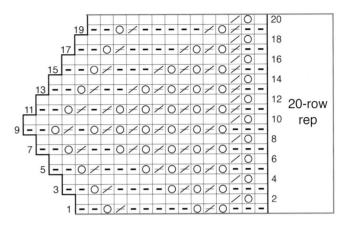

FLOWING LACE EDGING CHART

STITCH KEY

☐	K on RS
–	K on WS
⊙	Yo
╱	K2tog on RS
⁄	K2tog on WS

Falling Leaves Edging

Falling Leaves Edging (8 sts, inc to 20 sts)

Cast on 8 sts.

Row 1 (RS): K5, yo, k1, yo, k2—10 sts.

Row 2: P6, kfb, k3—11 sts.

Row 3: K4, p1, k2, yo, k1, yo, k3—13 sts.

Row 4: P8, kfb, k4—14 sts.

Row 5: K4, p2, k3, yo, k1, yo, k4—16 sts.

Row 6: P10, kfb, k5—17 sts.

Row 7: K4, p3, k4, yo, k1, yo, k5—19 sts.

Row 8: P12, kfb, k6—20 sts.

Row 9: K4, p4, ssk, k7, k2tog, k1—18 sts.

Row 10: P10, kfb, k7—19 sts.

Row 11: K4, p5, ssk, k5, k2tog, k1—17 sts.

Row 12: P8, kfb, k2, p1, k5—18 sts.

Row 13: K4, p1, k1, p4, ssk, k3, k2tog, k1—16 sts.

Row 14: P6, kfb, k3, p1, k5—17 sts.

Row 15: K4, p1, k1, p5, ssk, k1, k2tog, k1—15 sts.

Row 16: P4, kfb, k4, p1, k5—16 sts.

Row 17: K4, p1, k1, p6, sk2p, k1—14 sts.

Row 18: Bind off 6 sts pwise, p4 (including st on RH needle from bind-off), k4—8 sts.

Rep Rows 1–18 for pat.

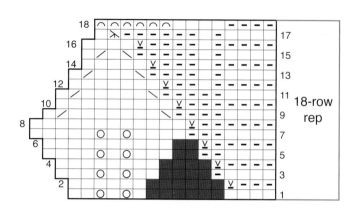

FALLING LEAVES EDGING CHART

18-row rep

STITCH KEY

☐	K on RS, p on WS
–	P on RS, k on WS
O	Yo
⊻	Kfb on WS
╱	K2tog
╲	Ssk
⋉	Sk2p
⌒	Bind off
■	No st

Meandering Lace Edging

Meandering Lace Edging (6 sts, inc to 13)
Cast on 6 sts.

Row 1 (WS): Knit.

Row 2 (RS): K2, yo, k2tog, yo, k2—7 sts.

Row 3: K2, [yo, k1] twice, yo, k2tog, k1—9 sts.

Row 4: K2, yo, k2tog, yo, k3, yo, k2—11 sts.

Row 5: K2, yo, k5, yo, k1, yo, k2tog, k1—13 sts.

Row 6: K2, yo, k2tog, yo, ssk, k3, k2tog, yo, k2.

Row 7: K3, yo, ssk, k1, k2tog, yo, k2, yo, k2tog, k1.

Row 8: K2, yo, k2tog, k2, yo, sk2p, yo, k4.

Row 9: Bind off 7 sts, k3 (including st on needle after bind-off), yo, k2tog, k1—6 sts.

Rep Rows 2–9 for pat.

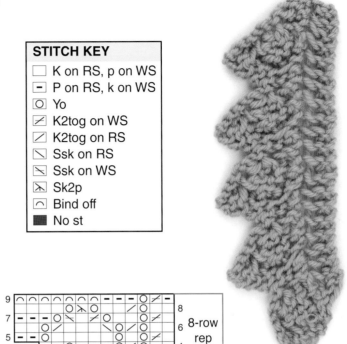

STITCH KEY

☐	K on RS, p on WS
─	P on RS, k on WS
○	Yo
⟋	K2tog on WS
⟋	K2tog on RS
⟍	Ssk on RS
⟍	Ssk on WS
⟑	Sk2p
⌒	Bind off
■	No st

MEANDERING LACE EDGING CHART

Ruffle

Ruffle (multiple of 3 sts)
With RS facing, pick up and knit a multiple of 3 sts along edge of project.

Row 1 (WS): P3, *yo, p3; rep from * to end.

Row 2 (RS): K3, *knit into (front, back, front, back) of yo, k3; rep from * to end.

Rows 3–12: Work in St st.

Bind off very loosely.

Plug & Play Cowls

Now it's time to pick your textures and the cowl you like best from these six stunning designs by Beth Whiteside. You can follow the patterns as written in this section, or refer back to Design Your Own Cowl on page 4 and customize as you like. Once you start you won't want to stop. Whether it's one stitch pattern repeated over and over or a sampler of all your favorite stitches, now is the time to showcase your skills and enhance your creative style.

Lace Sampler

About This Pattern

Three lace patterns are worked side by side which allows for combinations of patterns with different stitch repeats. Faggot stitch insertions flanked by purl channels separate the lace panels and create vertical lines.

When designing your own sampler, keep it simple by using patterns with row repeats that are the same or multiples of the same number, as with the patterns worked in this sampler: Diagonal Madeira Lace, Hourglass Lace (both 8-row repeats) and Mira Lace (a 16-row repeat).

Make sure your lace patterns have the same number of rows per inch, or your piece will be distorted!

Skill Level

■■■□ INTERMEDIATE

Finished Measurements

Before joining

Width: 16 inches
Length: 42 inches

Materials

- Universal Yarn Deluxe Worsted Superwash (worsted weight; 100% superwash wool; 220 yds/ 100g per ball): 3 balls sangria #737

  4 MEDIUM

- Size 9 (5.5mm) needles or size needed to obtain gauge

Gauge

15 sts and 24 rows = 4 inches/10cm in Hourglass Lace pat (blocked).

Special Abbreviation

Slip marker (sm): Slip markers to RH needle when you come to them.

Pattern Stitches

Diagonal Madeira Lace (multiple of 4 sts + 8)
See page 19.

Hourglass Lace (multiple of 6 sts + 8)
See page 26.

Mira Lace (multiple of 8 sts + 2)
See page 29.

Zigzag Trellis (5-st panel)
See page 19.

Designer Tip

Don't have a row counter? Keep track of the number of rows you've worked by placing a marker every time you finish 1 repeat of the Mira Lace pattern (2 repeats of the other patterns). Count how many rows there are above the marker and you will know which pattern row you need to work next!

Cowl

Cast on 70 sts.

Knit 4 rows.

Establish pats as follows:

Row 1 (RS): K2, p1 (selvage sts), pm, work 16 sts in Diagonal Madeira Lace, pm, work 5-st Zigzag Trellis panel, pm, work 20 sts in Hourglass pat, pm, work 5-st Zigzag Trellis panel, pm, work 18 sts in Mira Lace, pm, p1, k2 (selvage sts).

Row 2 (WS): K3, sm, work Mira Lace to marker, sm, work 5-st Zigzag Trellis panel, sm, work Hourglass Lace to marker, sm, work 5-st Zigzag Trellis panel, sm, work Diagonal Madeira Lace to marker, sm, k3.

Continue in established pats until piece measures 42 inches, ending with Row 15.

Knit 4 rows.

Bind off loosely.

Finishing

Weave in ends.

Wet-block to finished measurements.

Mark a point 16 inches from end along 1 long side. Using invisible seam (see page 62), sew short end of rectangle to long side between marker and end. ●

STITCH KEY
- ☐ K on RS, p on WS
- ⊟ P on RS, k on WS
- ⊠ P1-tbl on WS
- ◯ Yo
- ╱ K2tog
- ╲ Ssk
- ⋏ Sk2p

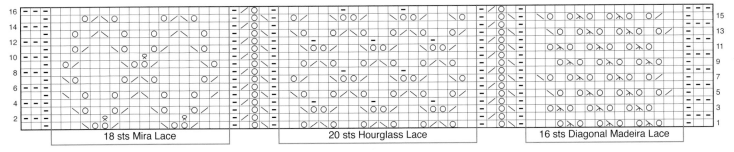

18 sts Mira Lace   20 sts Hourglass Lace   16 sts Diagonal Madeira Lace

LACE SAMPLER CHART

Roman Stripe Moebius

About This Pattern

Roman Lace is a reversible 14-row stitch pattern. The patterning on the first 7 rows flips, changing sides for the second 7 rows. That makes it a perfect pattern for a moebius strip, a long rectangle that is given a half-twist before the ends are joined. Working an extra half-repeat makes the patterns match up perfectly after grafting, creating a wearable cowl with only one surface!

Skill Level

 INTERMEDIATE

Finished Measurements

Width: 12 inches
Circumference: 40 inches

Materials

- Universal Yarn Wisdom Yarns Poems (worsted weight; 100% wool; 109 yds/50g per ball): 3 balls bramble #577
- Size 10½ (6.5mm) needles or size needed to obtain gauge
- Size K/10½ (6.5mm) crochet hook

Gauge

10 sts and 16 rows = 4 inches/10cm in Roman Lace pat.

To save time, take time to check gauge.

Pattern Stitch

Roman Lace (any number of sts)
See page 9.

Special Technique

Garter St Graft: Join live sts as for Kitchener st (see page 62), but work steps 2 and 3 as follows: **Step 2:** Insert tapestry needle into first st on back needle as if to knit. Draw yarn through st and slip st off knitting needle. **Step 3:** Insert needle into the next st on same (back) needle as if to purl, leaving st on knitting needle.

Pattern Notes

Cowl is worked as a rectangle. The piece is given a half-twist, then the cast-on row is grafted to the last row to form a moebius strip.

Slip first stitch of each row purlwise and knit last stitch. These edge stitches are not included as part of the Roman Lace pattern.

Cowl

Using provisional cast-on (see page 62), cast on 32 sts.

Row 1: Sl 1, work Roman Lace to last st, k1.

Slipping first st of every row and knitting last st, continue in Roman Lace pat until piece measures 40 inches, ending with Row 5.

Cut yarn, leaving a 45-inch tail.

Finishing

Remove crochet chain from cast-on and transfer live sts to 2nd needle. Give cast-on end a half twist. Holding needle with cast-on sts in front, join ends tog using tail and Garter St Graft .

Weave in ends. ●

Textured Sampler Cowl

About This Pattern

Samplers are a great way to try out different stitch patterns. This cowl's "linked chain" effect was created by working Twisted Rib between pattern stitch sections. Widen or narrow your chains by working more or fewer pattern repeats, using the pattern with the largest stitch repeat to determine the final stitch count.

When using pattern stitches in sequence, you can choose patterns that all have the same stitch multiples, increase and decrease stitches as needed between the patterns, or use a cast-on number that will accommodate several pattern multiples. The pattern stitch section of this cowl has 38 stitches, so any pattern that is a multiple of 4 stitches + 2 or 6 stitches + 2 can be used, as can any even-numbered pattern. A little creative rearrangement (such as moving 1 stitch to each selvage) can enable you to use other pattern repeats, as with the 12-stitch Pythagorean pattern section.

Skill Level

 INTERMEDIATE

Finished Measurements

Width: 7–9 inches
Circumference: 70 inches

Materials

- Universal Yarn Deluxe Worsted Superwash (worsted weight; 100% superwash wool; 220 yds/ 100g per ball): 3 balls nitrox blue #716
- Size 5 (3.75mm) needles or size needed to obtain gauge
- Size 8 (5mm) needles or 3 sizes larger than gauge needle
- Size 10½ (6.5mm) needles or 6 sizes larger than gauge needle (for Threaded St pat only)
- Size H/8 (5mm) crochet hook

4 MEDIUM

Gauge

26 sts and 40 rows = 4 inches/10cm in Twisted Rib using smaller needle.

To save time, take time to check gauge.

Special Abbreviations

Make 1 (M1): Insert LH needle from front to back under horizontal strand between last st worked and next st on LH needle, knit through back of resulting loop.

Wrap 2 (4): Sl 2 (4) sts to cn, wrap yarn around sts on cn once, k2 (4) from cn.

Slip marker (sm): Slip marker to RH needle.

Pattern Stitches

Twisted Rib (odd number of sts)

Row 1 (RS): K1-tbl, *p1, k1-tbl; rep from * to end.

Row 2: P1, *k1-tbl, p1; rep from * to end.

Rep Rows 1 and 2 for pat.

Roman St (even number of sts)

See page 11.

Threaded St (even number of sts)

Note: 2 needle sizes are used for this st pat. For purposes of this project, they are referred to as "larger needle" (which is the needle size used for all the pat-st sections in this project), and "largest needle," which should be 3 sizes larger.

Row 1 (RS): With larger needle, knit.

Rows 2 and 4: With largest needle, purl.

Row 3: With larger needle, *insert RH needle pwise through first st, knit 2nd st and leave on needle, knit first st tbl, slide both sts off LH needle; rep from * to end.

Row 5: With larger needle, k1, *insert RH needle pwise through first st, knit 2nd st and leave on needle, knit first st tbl, slide both sts off LH needle; rep from * to last st, k1.

Rep Rows 2–5 for pat.

Rosette St (multiple of 2 sts + 2)
See page 13.

Diagonal Scallop (multiple of 4 sts + 6)
See page 18.

Little Knots (multiple of 6 sts + 2)
See page 22.

Little Smocking (multiple of 6 sts + 8)
See page 27.

Pythagorean (multiple of 12 sts)
See page 36.

Pattern Notes
Project is worked by alternating 9-inch pattern-stitch sections (worked with larger needles) with 1 inch of Twisted Rib (worked with smaller needles).
Note: *The largest needle is used only for working the Threaded Stitch pattern.*

The pattern stitches are all worked with an even number of stitches, while the Rib Section has an odd number of stitches. When switching sections, decrease by working p2tog at some point in the first row of Twisted Rib and increase by working a Make 1 at some point in the first pattern row.

The 4-stitch selvages are worked with 1 stitch at each end in garter stitch and 3 stitches in Twisted Rib.

Cowl
With larger needles and using provisional cast-on method (see page 62), cast on 46 sts.

Roman St Section

Row 1 (WS): K1, k1-tbl, p1, k1-tbl (4-st selvage), pm, work Row 4 of Roman St pat across 38 sts, pm, k1-tbl, p1, k1-tbl, k1 (4-st selvage).

Row 2 (RS): K1, p1, k1-tbl, p1, sm, work Row 5 of Roman St pat to marker, sm, p1, k1-tbl, p1, k1.

Maintaining 4-st selvage at each side, continue working Roman St pat between markers until piece measures 8½ inches, ending with Row 4 of Roman St pat.

Rib Section

Switch to smaller needles.

Dec row (RS): Work 4-st selvage, then continue working Twisted Rib to last st and *at the same time,* dec 1 st, k1—45 sts.

Knitting first and last sts, work even in Twisted Rib for approx 1 inch, ending with a RS row.

Diagonal Scallop Section

Switch to larger needles.

Inc row (WS): Work 4-st selvage, sm; increasing 1 st, work Row 1 of Diagonal Scallop pat to marker, sm; work 4-st selvage—46 sts.

Maintaining 4-st selvage at each side, continue working Diagonal Scallop pat between markers until section measures 9 inches, ending with a WS row.

Rib Section

Rep Rib Section, beg with a RS row and ending with a WS row—45 sts.

Rosette St Section

Switch to larger needles.

Inc row (RS): Work 4-st selvage, sm; increasing 1 st, work Row 1 of Rosette St to marker, sm; work 4-st selvage—46 sts.

Maintaining 4-st selvage at each side, continue working Rosette St between markers until section measures 9 inches, ending with a RS row.

Rib Section

Rep Rib Section, beg with a WS row and ending with a RS row—45 sts.

Threaded St Section

Switch to largest needles.

Inc row (WS): Work 4-st selvage, sm; increasing 1 st, purl to marker, sm; work 4-st selvage—46 sts.

Maintaining 4-st selvage at each side and beg with Row 3 of Threaded St pat, continue working Threaded St pat between markers (alternating needle sizes as instructed) until section measures 9 inches, ending with a RS row.

Rib Section

Rep Rib Section, beg and ending with a WS row—45 sts.

Pythagorean Section

Note: *To accommodate the 12-st pat rep, the selvage is increased to 5 sts, leaving 36 pat sts in center.*

Switch to larger needles.

Inc row (RS): Shifting marker positions as indicated, work 4-st selvage, k1-tbl, pm; increasing 1 st, work Row 1 of Pythagorean pat to last 5 sts, pm; k1-tbl, work 4-st selvage—46 sts.

Maintaining 5-st selvage at each side, continue working Pythagorean pat between markers for 55 rows (2 pat reps), ending with Row 28.

Rib Section

Rep Rib Section, beg and ending with a RS row—45 sts.

Little Knots Section

Switch to larger needles.

Inc row (WS): Shifting marker positions as indicated, work 4-st selvage, pm; increasing 1 st, work Row 1 of Little Knots pat to last 4 sts, pm; work 4-st selvage—46 sts.

Maintaining 4-st selvage at each side, continue working Little Knots pat between markers until section measures 9 inches, ending with a RS row.

Rib Section
Rep Rib Section, beg and ending with a WS row—45 sts.

Little Smocking Section
Switch to larger needles.

Inc row (RS): Work 4-st selvage, sm; increasing 1 st, work Row 1 of Little Smocking pat to marker, sm; work 4-st selvage—46 sts.

Maintaining 4-st selvage at each side, continue working Little Smocking pat between markers until section measures 9 inches, ending with Row 4 or 8.

Rib Section
Rep Rib Section, beg with a RS row and ending with a WS row—45 sts.

Switch to larger needles.

Inc row (RS): Work 4-st selvage, sm; increasing 1 st, knit to marker, sm; work 4-st selvage.

Cut yarn, leaving a 36-inch tail.

Finishing
Transfer sts to scrap yarn, then block to measurements.

Transfer sts back to needle.

Unzip crochet chain from cast-on and transfer live sts to 2nd needle.

Holding needle with cast-on sts in front and using tail, graft ends tog using Kitchener st (see page 62).

Weave in ends. ●

Designer Tip
Patterns that are primarily stockinette stitch will tend to roll and will therefore require more aggressive blocking to lie flat than those that alternate knit and purl stitches throughout the fabric. Wet-block and pin them to size.

Cabled Cowl

About This Pattern

This cowl is worked flat and features a center lattice cable panel flanked by simple 2/2 cable panels that are mirrored on either side. The 2/2 cables are turned on the same rows for all of the patterns, making it easier to know where you are. The 4-row side cable panel repeats are worked twice for each 8-row repeat of the center lattice panel.

If you've never worked from a chart before, this cowl is a nice introduction. All the action happens on right-side rows; on wrong-side rows, you work all stitches as they present themselves, knitting the knit stitches and purling the purl stitches.

When designing your own cowl and placing patterns side by side, be sure to check that their row gauges are compatible. If they don't each have the same number of rows per inch, they won't give you the same number of inches over a number of rows—and your fabric may be distorted in unexpected ways.

Skill Level

 INTERMEDIATE

Finished Measurements

Width: 7 inches
Length: 25¼ inches (unbuttoned)

Materials

- Universal Yarn Deluxe Worsted Superwash (worsted weight; 100% superwash wool; 220 yds/ 100g per ball): 2 balls burrow #731
- Size 8 (5mm) needles or size needed to obtain gauge
- Cable needle
- 5 (⅞-inch) buttons

Gauge

32 sts and 30 rows = 4 inches/10cm in Basket Lattice Cable pat.

To save time, take time to check gauge.

Special Abbreviations

2 over 2 Right Cross (2/2 RC): Sl 2 to cn and hold in back, k2, k2 from cn.

2 over 2 Left Cross (2/2 LC): Sl 2 to cn and hold in front, k2, k2 from cn.

2 over 1 Right Purl Cross (2/1 RPC): Sl 1 to cn and hold in back, k2, p1 from cn.

2 over 1 Left Purl Cross (2/1 LPC): Sl 2 to cn and hold in front, p1, k2 from cn.

Pattern Stitches

Basket Lattice Cable (multiple of 6 sts + 8)
See page 24.

Left Cable Panel (10-st panel)

Rows 1 and 3 (WS): P1, k2, p4, k2, p1.

Row 2 (RS): K1, p2, 2/2 LC, p2, k1.

Row 4: K1, p2, k4, p2, k1.

Rep Rows 1–4 for pat.

Right Cable Panel (10-st panel)

Rows 1 and 3 (WS): P1, k2, p4, k2, p1.

Row 2 (RS): K1, p2, 2/2 RC, p2, k1.

Row 4: K1, p2, k4, p2, k1.

Rep Rows 1–4 for pat.

Pattern Notes

Chart shows vertical placement of Basket Lattice Cable, flanked by Left and Right Cable Panels.

The 2 selvage stitches at each side are worked as 1 garter stitch (at the outer edges) and 1 stockinette stitch.

Cowl

Cast on 56 sts.

Buttonhole Band

Row 1 and all WS rows: K1, p2, k2, p4, k2, p1, [k2, p4] 5 times, k2, p1, k2, p4, k2, p2, k1.

Row 2 (RS): K3, p2, 2/2 LC, p2, k1, [p2, 2/2 LC] 5 times, p2, k1, p2, 2/2 RC, p2, k3.

Row 4: K3, p2, k4, p2, k1, [p2, k4] 5 times, p2, k1, p2, k4, p2, k3.

Row 6 (buttonhole row): K3, p2, k2tog, yo, k2, p2, k1, [p2, k2tog, yo, k2, p2] 5 times, p2, k1, p2, k2, yo, ssk, p2, p2, k3.

Rows 8 and 10: Rep Row 4.

Body

Establish pats as follows:

Row 1 (WS): K1, p1 (selvage sts), pm, work Row 1 of Left Cable Panel, pm, work Basket Lattice Cable across 32 sts, pm, work Right Cable Panel, pm, p1, k1 (selvage sts).

Row 2 (RS): Slipping markers when you come to them and working Row 2 of each pat, k2, work Right Cable Panel, work Basket Lattice Cable across 32 sts, work Left Cable Panel, k2.

Work even in established pats until piece measures approx 21¼ inches, ending with Row 3 of Lattice Cable.

Button Band

Rows 1, 3, 5 and 7 (RS): K3, p2, k4, p2, k1, [p2, k4] 5 times, p2, k1, p2, k4, p2, k3.

Row 2 and all WS rows: K1, p2, k2, p4, k2, p1, [k2, p4] 5 times, k2, p1, k2, p4, k2, p2, k1.

Row 9: K3, p2, 2/2 LC, p2, k1, [p2, 2/2 LC] 5 times, p2, k1, p2, 2/2 RC, p2, k3.

Bind off.

Finishing

Weave in ends.

Block to finished measurements.

Sew buttons opposite buttonholes. ●

STITCH KEY
- ☐ K on RS, p on WS
- − P on RS, k on WS
- ☉ Yo
- ◿ K2tog
- ◺ Ssk
- 2/1 LPC
- 2/1 RPC
- 2/2 LC
- 2/2 RC

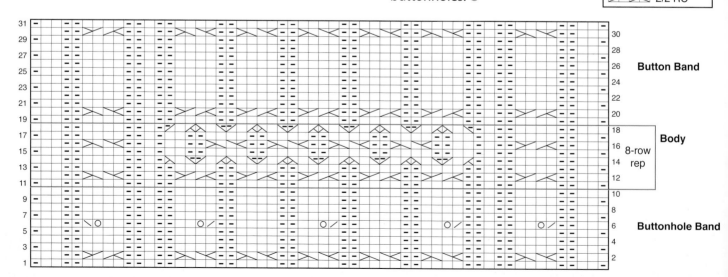

CABLED COWL CHART

Button Band

Body — 8-row rep

Buttonhole Band

Pleated Scarflette

About This Pattern

Make the edging the focal point of your piece with this Pleated Scarflette. Swedish Check and garter stitch are the supporting cast, while I-cord loops tie it all together.

Skill Level

 INTERMEDIATE

Finished Measurements

Width: 6 inches
Length: 23½ inches

Materials

- Universal Yarn Deluxe Worsted Superwash (worsted weight; 100% superwash wool; 220 yds/100g per ball): 2 balls butter #708
- Size 6 (4mm) double-point and 24-inch circular needles or size needed to obtain gauge
- 2 (1½-inch) round buttons or toggle buttons
- Crochet hook

4 MEDIUM

Gauge

22 sts and 36 rows = 4 inches/10cm in Swedish Check pat.

To save time, take time to check gauge.

Special Abbreviation

12-Stitch Left Pleat (12-St LP): Slip 6 sts to dpn and hold in front; working 1 st from main needle tog with 1 st from dpn, k2tog 6 times.

Special Technique

I-Cord: With 3 sts on dpn, *k3, do not turn, slide sts to other end of dpn; rep from * until cord is desired length.

Pattern Stitches

Seed St (odd number of sts)
See page 11.

Swedish Check (multiple of 4 sts + 2)
See page 16.

Pattern Notes

Scarflette is worked back and forth in rows. Circular needle is used to accommodate the large number of stitches. Do not join.

I-cord button loops may be worked separately and sewn in place instead of being worked into the fabric. If using smaller buttons, sew I-cord together to desired loop size.

Scarflette

Pleats
Cast on 215 sts.

Work 2 rows in Seed St.

Knitting first and last st of every row, work 10 rows in St st.

Next row (RS): K4, *12-St LP, k3; rep from * to last st, k1—131 sts.

Knit 3 rows, and on last row, inc 5 sts evenly spaced across—136 sts.

The scarflette uses left-pulled pleats, but you can easily work right-pulled pleats instead by holding the double-point needle with the slipped stitches in back of the main needle instead of in front. Or, if designing your own scarflette, create inverted and box pleats by alternating left and right pleats.

Using dpn, pick up and knit 3 sts in 4 rows at first marked button-loop position.

Work I-cord for 6 inches; cut yarn, leaving an 8-inch tail.

Working in line with column where sts were picked up, use crochet hook to pull each live st on needle, 1 by 1, through to WS, then place sts back on dpn. Pull yarn tail through to WS. Bind off.

Sew parallel cords tog for approx 1½ inches, leaving open loop at end. Tack joined cords to scarflette, letting loop hang over the edge.

Work 2nd button loop at 2nd marked position.

Sew buttons opposite button loops.

Weave in ends. ●

Center

Set-up row (RS): K1, work Swedish Check pat to last st, k1.

Maintaining first and last sts in garter st, complete 3 [8-row] reps of Swedish Check pat, then work Rows 1–4.

Knit 3 rows.

Bind off.

Finishing

Weave in ends.

Wet-block to finished measurements, pinning pleats to shape.

Button Loops

Mark placement for 2 loops approx 1½ inches in from selvage, with the first just above garter rows on pleat side and the 2nd just below garter rows at neck edge (see photograph).

Lace Shoulderette

About This Pattern

It's all in the edging on this circular shoulderette. The stitch patterns have been adapted to be worked from the top down and in the round; the right side will always be facing you.

When the frill is worked from the bottom up, extra stitches are cast on with all the other pattern stitches and dropped at the top of the edging, widening the fabric. The same effect can be created when working top down: Work yarn-over increases at the beginning of the edging section, and drop them off the needle as you bind off. Chain stitches between bound-off stitches add the necessary extra width to the fabric.

Skill Level

■■■□ INTERMEDIATE

Finished Measurements

Length: 15½ inches
Lower edge circumference: 44 inches

Materials

- Universal Yarn Deluxe Worsted Superwash (worsted weight; 100% superwash wool; 220 yds/100g per ball): 3 balls petit pink #723

  4 MEDIUM

- Size 6 (4mm) 16- and 24-inch circular needles or size needed to obtain gauge

Gauge

20 sts and 26 rnds = 4 inches/10cm in Cat's Eye pat.

To save time, take time to check gauge.

Pattern Stitches

Note: Instructions for all pat sts have been converted from flat to circular method of working.

Twisted Rib (even number of sts)

Rnd 1: *K1-tbl, p1; rep from * around.

Rnd 2: *K1, p1-tbl; rep from * around.

Rep Rnds 1 and 2 for pat.

Italian Chain Rib (multiple of 6 sts)

Rnd 1: *P2, k4; rep from * around.

Rnd 2: *P2, k2tog, 2yo, ssk; rep from * around.

Rnd 3: *P2, k1, kfb into 2yo, k1; rep from * around.

Rnd 4: *P2, yo, ssk, k2tog, yo; rep from * around.

Rep Rnds 1–4 for pat.

Cat's Eye (multiple of 4 sts)

Note: St count will inc on Rnds 1 and 3 and dec back to original count on Rnds 2 and 4. On Rnds 3 and 4, remove and replace beg-of-rnd marker as necessary to work pat sts.

Rnd 1: *K2, 2yo, k2; rep from * around.

Rnd 2: *K2tog, (k1, p1) into 2yo, k2tog; rep from * around.

Rnd 3: *2yo, k4; rep from * around.

Rnd 4: *(K1, p1) into 2yo, k2tog twice; rep from * around.

Rep Rnds 1–4 for pat.

Special Abbreviations

Double yarn over (2yo): Wrap yarn around needle twice. On following rnd, work 2 sts into the long loop created by the 2yo as instructed.

Chain-6 (Ch-6): [Yo RH needle, pass st over] 6 times.

Pattern Notes

Shoulderette is worked in the round from the top down.

Cast on using shorter circular needle, and then change to longer needle when there are enough stitches to do so.

Shoulderette

Cast on 144 sts, pm for beg of rnd and join, taking care not to twist sts.

Work 3 rnds Twisted Rib.

Work Italian Chain Rib until piece measures 4¼ inches, ending with Rnd 4.

Inc rnd: *K1, p1, kfb; rep from * around—192 sts.

Work 5 rnds in Twisted Rib.

Work Cat's Eye pat until piece measures approx 10½ inches, ending with Rnd 2 or 4.

Work 6 rnds in Twisted Rib.

Frill

Inc rnd: *[K1-tbl, p1, yo] twice, k1-tbl, p1; rep from * around—256 sts.

Rnd 1: *[K1, p1-tbl, p1] twice, k1, p1-tbl; rep from * around.

Rnd 2: *[K1-tbl, p2] twice, k1-tbl, p1; rep from * around.

Rep last 2 rnds until piece measures approx 15 inches or desired length, ending with Rnd 1.

Bind-off rnd: Bind off 1 st (1 st on RH needle following bind-off), *drop next st off needle, Ch-6, bind off 2 sts, drop next st off needle, Ch-6, bind off 4 sts; rep from * around.

Unravel dropped sts to yo on Inc rnd.

Finishing

Weave in ends.

Block. ●

Designer Tip

When converting instructions from flat to circular, draw patterns out on graph paper. It's an easy way to see how decreases translate from wrong side to right side, which stitches interact with which, and whether the extra stitches at the sides are "balancing" stitches that can be removed when working in the round.

Knitting Basics

Long-Tail Cast-On

Make a slip knot on the right needle.

Place the thumb and index finger of your left hand between the yarn ends with the long yarn end over your thumb, and the strand from the yarn ball over your index finger. Close your other fingers over the strands to hold them against your palm. Spread your thumb and index fingers apart and draw the yarn into a V.

Place the needle in front of the strand around your thumb and bring it underneath this strand. Carry the needle over and under the strand on your index finger.

Draw the strand through the loop on your thumb. Drop the loop from your thumb and draw up the strand to form a stitch on the knitting needle.

Repeat until you have cast on the number of stitches indicated in the pattern.

Knit (k)

With yarn in back, insert the right needle from front to back into the next stitch on the left needle.

Bring the yarn under and over the right needle, wrapping the yarn counterclockwise around the needle.

Use the right needle to pull the loop through the stitch.

Slide the stitch off the left needle.

Purl (p)

With yarn in front, insert the right needle from back to front into the next stitch on the left needle.

Wrap the yarn counterclockwise around the right needle.

Use the right needle to pull the loop through the stitch and to the back.

Slide the stitch off left needle.

Bind Off

Binding Off (knit)

Knit the first two stitches on the left needle. Insert the left needle into the first stitch worked on the right needle, then lift that first stitch over the second stitch and off the right needle. Knit the next stitch and repeat.

When one stitch remains on the right needle, cut the yarn and draw the tail through the last stitch to fasten off.

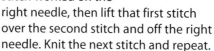

Binding Off (purl)

Purl the first two stitches on the left needle.

Insert the left needle into the first stitch worked on the right needle, then lift the first stitch over the second stitch and off the right needle. Purl the next stitch and repeat.

When one stitch remains on the right needle, cut the yarn and draw the tail through the last stitch to fasten off.

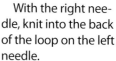

Increase (inc)

Bar Increase (knit: kfb)

Knit the next stitch but do not remove the original stitch from the left needle.

Insert the right needle behind the left needle and knit into the back of the same stitch.

Slip the original stitch off the left needle.

Bar Increase (purl: pfb)

Purl the next stitch but do not remove the original stitch from the left needle.

Insert the right needle behind the left needle and purl into the back of the same stitch.

Slip the original stitch off the left needle.

Make 1 With Left Twist (M1L)

Insert the left needle from front to back under the strand that runs between the stitch on the right needle and the stitch on the left needle.

With the right needle, knit into the back of the loop on the left needle.

To make this increase on the purl side, insert left needle in same manner and purl into the back of the loop.

Make 1 With Right Twist (M1R)

Insert the left needle from back to front under the strand that runs between the stitch on the right needle and the stitch on the left needle.

With the right needle, knit into the front of the loop on the left needle.

To make this increase on the purl side, insert left needle in same manner and purl into the front of the loop.

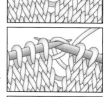

Make 1 With Backward Loop

Use your thumb to make a backward loop of yarn over the right needle. Slip the loop from your thumb onto the needle and pull to tighten.

Decrease (dec)

Knit 2 Together (k2tog)

Insert the right needle through the next two stitches on the left needle as if to knit. Knit these two stitches together as one.

Purl 2 Together (p2tog)

Insert the right needle through the next two stitches on the left needle as if to purl. Purl these two stitches together as one.

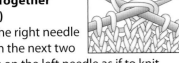

Slip, Slip, Knit (ssk)

Slip the next two stitches, one at a time, from the left needle to the right needle as if to knit.

Insert the left needle through both slipped stitches in front of the right needle.

Knit these two stitches together.

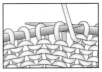

Slip, Slip, Purl (ssp)

Slip the next two stitches, one at a time, from the left needle to the right needle as if to knit.

Slip these stitches back to the left needle keeping them twisted.

Purl these two stitches together through their back loops.

Standard Abbreviations

[ ] work instructions within brackets as many times as directed

( ) work instructions within parentheses in the place directed

** repeat instructions following the asterisks as directed

* repeat instructions following the single asterisk as directed

" inch(es)

approx approximately

beg begin/begins/beginning

CC contrasting color

ch chain stitch

cm centimeter(s)

cn cable needle

dec(s) decrease/decreases/ decreasing

dpn(s) double-point needle(s)

g gram(s)

inc(s) increase/increases/ increasing

k knit

k2tog knit 2 stitches together

kfb knit in front and back

kwise knitwise

LH left hand

m meter(s)

MC main color

mm millimeter(s)

oz ounce(s)

p purl

p2tog purl 2 stitches together

pat(s) pattern(s)

pm place marker

psso pass slipped stitch over

pwise purlwise

rem remain/remains/ remaining

rep(s) repeat(s)

rev St st reverse stockinette stitch

RH right hand

rnd(s) rounds

RS right side

skp slip 1 knitwise, knit 1, pass slipped stitch over—a left-leaning decrease

sk2p slip 1 knitwise, knit 2 together, pass slipped stitch over the stitch from the knit-2-together decrease—a left-leaning double decrease

sl slip

sl 1 kwise slip 1 knitwise

sl 1 pwise slip 1 purlwise

sl st(s) slipped stitch(es)

ssk slip 2 stitches, 1 at a time, knitwise; knit these stitches together through the back loops—a left-leaning decrease

st(s) stitch(es)

St st stockinette stitch

tbl through back loop(s)

tog together

WS wrong side

wyib with yarn in back

wyif with yarn in front

yd(s) yard(s)

yfwd yarn forward

yo (yo's) yarn over(s)

Standard Yarn Weight System

Categories of yarn, gauge ranges, and recommended needle sizes

Yarn Weight Symbol & Category Names	0 LACE	1 SUPER FINE	2 FINE	3 LIGHT	4 MEDIUM	5 BULKY	6 SUPER BULKY
Type of Yarns in Category	Fingering, 10-Count Crochet Thread	Sock, Fingering, Baby	Sport, Baby	DK, Light Worsted	Worsted, Afghan, Aran	Chunky, Craft, Rug	Bulky, Roving
Knit Gauge Range* in Stockinette Stitch to 4 inches	33–40 sts**	27–32 sts	23–26 sts	21–24 sts	16–20 sts	12–15 sts	6–11 sts
Recommended Needle in Metric Size Range	1.5–2.25mm	2.25–3.25mm	3.25–3.75mm	3.75–4.5mm	4.5–5.5mm	5.5–8mm	8mm and larger
Recommended Needle U.S. Size Range	000 to 1	1 to 3	3 to 5	5 to 7	7 to 9	9 to 11	11 and larger

* GUIDELINES ONLY: The above reflect the most commonly used gauges and needle sizes for specific yarn categories.
** Lace weight yarns are often knitted on larger needles and hooks to create lacy, openwork patterns. Accordingly, a gauge range is difficult to determine. Always follow the gauge stated in your pattern.

Skill Levels

BEGINNER

Beginner projects for first-time knitters using basic stitches. Minimal shaping.

EASY

Easy projects using basic stitches, repetitive stitch patterns, simple color changes, and simple shaping and finishing.

INTERMEDIATE

Intermediate projects with a variety of stitches, mid-level shaping and finishing.

EXPERIENCED

Experienced projects using advanced techniques and stitches, detailed shaping and refined finishing.

Special Techniques

Kitchener Stitch

This method of weaving with two needles is used for the toes of socks and flat seams. To weave the edges together and form an unbroken line of stockinette stitch, divide all stitches evenly onto two knitting needles—one behind the other. Thread yarn into tapestry needle. Hold needles with wrong sides together and work from right to left as follows:

Step 1:

Insert tapestry needle into first stitch on front needle as to purl. Draw yarn through stitch, leaving stitch on knitting needle.

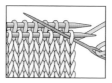

Step 2:

Insert tapestry needle into the first stitch on the back needle as to purl. Draw yarn through stitch and slip stitch off knitting needle.

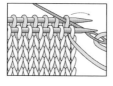

Step 3:

Insert tapestry needle into the next stitch on same (back) needle as to knit, leaving stitch on knitting needle.

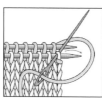

Step 4:

Insert tapestry needle into the first stitch on the front needle as to knit. Draw yarn through stitch and slip stitch off knitting needle.

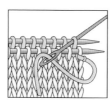

Step 5:

Insert tapestry needle into the next stitch on same (front) needle as to purl. Draw yarn through stitch, leaving stitch on knitting needle.

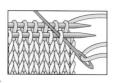

Repeat Steps 2 through 5 until one stitch is left on each needle. Then repeat Steps 2 and 4. Fasten off. Woven stitches should be the same size as adjacent knitted stitches.

Provisional Cast-On

The provisional cast-on has a variety of uses. It starts with a crochet chain on a crochet hook about the same size as the knitting needle. A chart is given below of crochet hooks that correspond most closely to knitting needle sizes.

Crochet Hook	Knitting Needle
E	4
F	5
G	6
H	8
I	9
J	10
K	10½

To work this type of cast-on, start with a crochet chain one or two stitches more than the number of stitches to be cast on for the pattern you are working. Since the edge is removed to work in the opposite direction the chain should be made with a contrasting color.

Once the chain is completed, with a knitting needle, pick up and knit in the back bar of each chain until the required number of stitches is on the needle. Continue to work the pattern as given in the instructions.

Instructions then indicate that the provisional cast-on be removed so the piece can be worked in the opposite direction. In this case, hold the work with the cast-on edge at the top. Undo one loop of the crochet chain, inserting the knitting needle into the stitch below the chain. (This stitch is on the original first row of knitting.) Continue to undo the crochet chain until all the stitches are on the needle. This provides a row of stitches ready to work in the opposite direction.

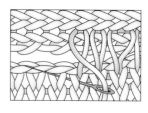

Invisible Seam

To sew a vertical edge to a horizontal edge, use a combination of the mattress stitch (vertical seaming method) and the horizontal seaming method. Work across one piece of fabric vertically, picking up the bars, and across the other piece horizontally, working under the point of the "v"s. When working stockinette stitch, for every third "v" point picked up, pick up 2 bars rather than one. For other stitch patterns, pinning the two pieces together will give a good indication of how to ease the two pieces together.

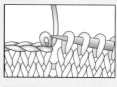

Photo Index

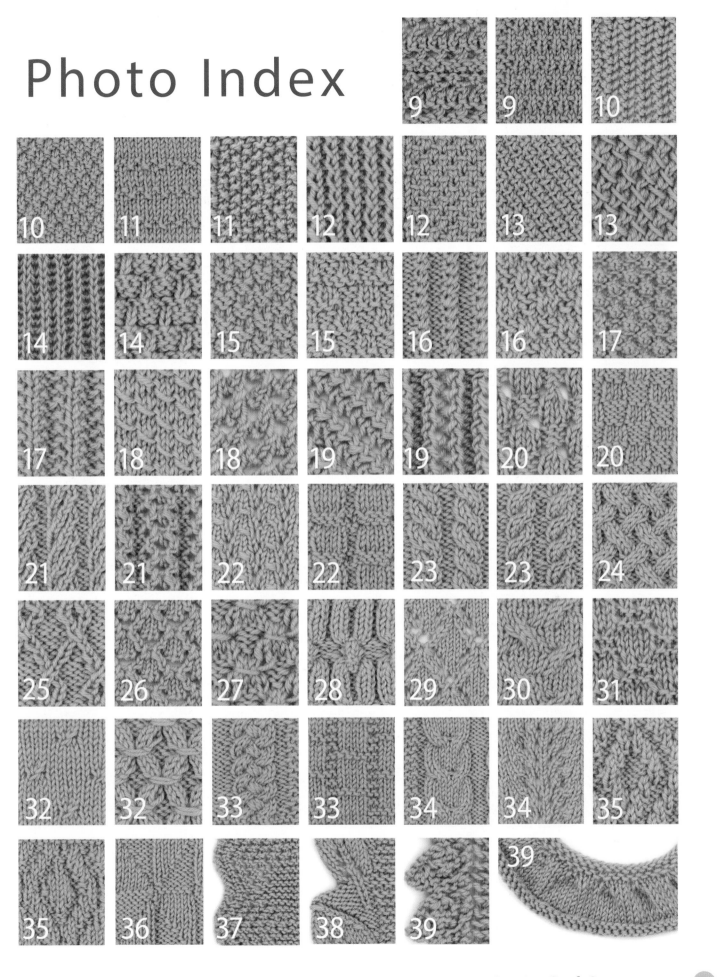

ISBN: 978-1-59635-962-8

1 2 3 4 5 6 7 8 9